ASSA

ASSAMESE DEMONOLOGY

A CULTURAL STUDY

First Edition 1906
Benudhar Rajhkowa

New Edition 2018
Edited by Tarl Warwick

COPYRIGHT AND DISCLAIMER

FOREWORD

This following little work is a fine example of Victorian Era academia; a good study of the region of Assam (in India, specifically the region not far above modern Bangladesh) and the various odd spirits said within the folklore present there to reside within. These spirits range from the literally deified to the fairly low, and from the mostly innocuous to the malevolent. Dozens of such entities are said, within local folklore, to exist. A fascinating study, since some of the Hindu deities themselves make an appearance within this lore.

Most studied here are the Dot and Khetar- both malevolent, after a fashion, but other odd entities are said to be even more negative. Some merely sicken or inconvenience- others kill outright, or hunt children, among other malevolent pass-times.

This edition of "Assamese Demonology" has been carefully edited for word usage and format. Care has been taken to retain all original intent and meaning.

CONTENTS

INTRODUCTION

CHAPTER I: AN ACCOUNT OF SPIRITS

CHAPTER II: INCANTATIONS AND EXPULSION OF SPIRITS

CHAPTER III: SUPPLEMANTARY NOTES

CHAPTER IV: STORIES

APPENDIX:

I: SONG OF ALAKHANI

II: INCANTATION USED IN WEAVING SPECTRAL THREAD

III: PRINCIPAL HAUNTED PLACES

IV: NOTABLE EXORCISTS

GLOSSARY

PREFACE

Like all other countries under the heavens, Assam has her indigenous ghosts. These pages are an attempt to describe their ways and habits, according to popular belief, with a view that they may be profitably used by all seekers after truth- the spiritualist and the mystic. They are a faithful record of what has fallen from the lips of the populace, Without the slightest varnish of my own.

The Assamese are a Hindu race and as such believe in the numerous Sanskrit deities of the heavens. Some of these deities have been however degraded to the position of hobgoblins. Others have been hurled from their proud, unapproachable region and placed in the rank and file of the spirit-kingdom.

The pure celestial deities may be passed over in this treatise and those alone will be noticed Who have anything to do in the arena of human life in their ordinary spheres. The astrological bodies again will not come under my re view. There are both benign and malign spirits as well as indifferent ones. Some of the spirits exercise double functions, while others do not. It is a striking fact that the generality of the Assamese spirits are malignant.

B. R.
Sibsagar, October, 1904.

INTRODUCTION

The author has asked me to write a brief introduction for 'his little book, and I do so gladly. The subject is a most interesting one, and although the author does not claim to have dealt with it on scientific lines, his pages will repay perusal. The book is a faithful record of popular beliefs in Assam in all their original quaintness. And for such a task, it would not be easy to find any one better qualified than the author.

W. J. REID.
Kohima, Assam.
September 27, 1904.

ASSAMESE DEMONOLOGY

CHAPTER I: AN ACCOUNT OF SPIRITS

It is impossible to attempt any classification of spirits-much less one based on natural history. I may, however, for the satisfaction of my readers, without entering into the niceties of distinction lay down broadly the following four territorial classes:

I Subterranean.
II Terrestrial.
III Aerial.
IV Calestial.

Terrestrial includes; (A) Aqueous; (B) Sylvan; (C) House hold. By far the largest number of spirits known to the Assamese fall under head II.

I begin with this class.

(A) Aqueous spirits- bak, dot, jakh, datial or jankakhoria, jalshai, and jalnarayan.

(1) Bak: He is fond of fish. His body emits an offensive smell which is translated to the very water over which he wanders. He catches fish by netting. He lives in a deserted tank. There is an Assamese proverb which runs thus:

Hahar oparat sial raja
Pota pukhutrit bak raja
A jackal is the lord of poultry.
A bak is supreme in a deserted tank.

(2) Dot: The word is derived from Sanskrit daitya, a demon. Of all the spirits, the. dot is most heard of among the

7

ASSAMESE DEMONOLOGY

Assamese. He leads people by all manner of inducements to any out-of-the-way place and there deals merciless blows on them. He however seldom kills a man. Sometimes he is known to visit a man at dawn in the form of familiar friend and leads him to the water-course, where he had set up his fishing trap the preceding evening, on the pretext of seeing if any fish have got in. But alas, the victim finds, when it is too late, that he has to deal with a most ungrateful wretch of a chum!

The dot is a slender but tall figure, measuring about 18 feet, with long fingers like spikes. He lives in channels, tanks, morasses, shaded out-of-the-way places overgrown with watery plants. He is jet-black in appearance, naked and has the several limbs of the body indistinguishable except the fingers which he exposes very prominently; in order to frighten his victim. He lives also in the midst of a bamboo grove. His body is exceedingly glutinous and has thus an advantage over his victim in a wrestle. Of all things that which is most dreaded by the dot is mustard grain. It is for this fact that mustard plays so important a part in the ceremonies of exorcism. I presume, it is avoided by the spirit; himself a glutinous body, on account of its slippery qualities which elude all attempts at a fast hold. The dot manifests himself first as an ordinary man, but gradually grows higher and higher till he vanishes altogether. The victim, at this sight, is frightened out of his wits, and the spirit taking advantage of his weakness of nerve at once possesses him. Sometimes he actually clasps the man in his arms and carries him off when he is solitary. The dots hair hangs about his head neglected and disordered. The hair of the female dot is similarly disheveled. She puts on tattered clothes. In the sight of his wife, the dot never dares to maltreat his, victim. In her absence he beats him mercilessly and sometimes forces his head into mud in a deserted tank, keeping his legs suspended in air. The dot neighs like a horse. He is powerless to approach a righteous man, much less do him any injury. Like bak, the dot also is a lover of fish.

He is afraid of a fish-hook and a reaping sickle. Of all the accompaniments of dot that are mentioned, the most curious is his spectral bag. This he always carries about under his armpit. It is by virtue of this bag that he exercises super-human powers. Without it he is but an ordinary mortal; It may be observed that a man sometimes succeeds in snatching this bag by force or inducement, and he thereupon places it for safety in a granary of mustard. Bereft of his wonderful talisman, the dot loses all powers and becomes a bound servant to the man. He works then like an ordinary human servant. He plows the field of his master, and faithfully does all other works that may be entrusted to him. But all the time he is on the look-out for his spectral bag, and when by an ingenious trick played in the absence of his master on the good wife he manages to get it at once he regains his powers and departs, whistling merrily, to his home to the bewilderment of his out-witted mistress. The spectral bag is made of net cloth In every other respect it has the appearance of an ordinary bag used by the Assamese for keeping their betel-leaves and areca-nuto. Little folks are seen here and there wear about their necks a fishing hook to scare away the dot.

(3) Jakh: He is a terrible spirit. He kills his victim by gnawing into his vital parts. He assumes the form of a large buffalo and splashes the water with his horns. He is sometimes seen roaming about in the company of domestic buffalos. It is the buffalo-herds who generally have encounters with this spirit or devil. A man under his possession bellows like a buffalo. This spirit is named mah-jakh (mah means a buffalo) to distinguish it from an ordinary jakh. There is another kind of jakh, called bioi-jakh which possesses a woman in child-birth.

(4) Datial or jankakharia: Datial literally means "living on the beach" while jankakharia means "living on the bank of a channel". This spirit lives near water-courses. He is a pagan spirit and is beyond the influence of incantations.

(5) Jalshai and jalnarayan: These two brother spirits preside over water as their names imply. Unlike a datial or jan-kakharia they are both Hindus by religion and do not murder a man though "they may punish him for transgressions."

(B) Sylvan Spirits:

(1) Chaman: He is noted for taciturnity. For this peculiar trait in his character he is always associated with the appellation "dumb". When possessed by him a man loses all power of speech. The name "chaman" is derived from the sham tree, his usual place of resort. He is also found in nahor or similar big trees in a deep forest. When a man happens to cut a branch of the tree, or passes urine under it, he is at once possessed.

(2) Bura-dangaria: It is a title of respect applied to an elderly Assamese gentleman. This spirit wears a magnificent turban like an Assamese gentleman and hence the name. Besides the turban he wears a wrapper. A dhuti hangs down below his waist. His clothes are white as marble. He is tall in stature, strongly built and looks like a full-blossomed rose. Of all the spirits it is bura-dangaria who is most religiously disposed. He attends at all religious assemblies among men. Nobody can with impunity fell a tree haunted by bura-dangaria without propitiating him. The offenders are scourged with bodily ailments. Sometimes it so happens that the tree which is out without propitiating bura-dangaria, maintains its inertia and never moves no matter what amount of force is brought to bear on it.

(3) Alakhani: This is a female spirit. She lives in the midst of a bamboo grove under a plant like a mushroom. This plant is about 8 inches high, and is called in Assamese alakhani bah" or the cell of alakhani. She is a frolicsome imp. Out she

goes trippingly on pleasure exursions and possesses any man whom she happens to come across. The female alakhani deals more frequently with men than the male one. The male imp, as might be expected, is more cruel and subjects his victim to extreme agony.

(4) Pisach: He lives in out-of-the-way filthy quarters.

(5) Phisoyani: The word is a corruption of pisitchani or female pisatch but is really applicable to a different spirit in no way connected with her. The spirit to which the word refers is execrable. She secretes her spittle, a frothy liquid, upon the leaf of a plant. Her spittle is a nuisance and is carefully avoided by men. When it perchance touches any part of the body there starts up immediately a cluster of fulsome itches.

(6) Daini: The word is derived from the Sanskrit dakini, an attendant of the goddess Kali. She is a. female spirit. Her chief characteristic is greediness. She is a, cannibal. Her greediness being at the highest tension her mouth waters and the lower lip protrudes as soon as she happens to see a man in front.

(7) Peret: On the death of a man the soul wanders about aimlessly for some time before a permanent abode is allotted to it. During this period it is known as peret. A man under the possession of this spirit suffers from itches, boils etc. He bears a disfigured body and a dejected mind. Hence any slovenly or melancholic person has come to be known by the word peretia (affected by peret.)

(8) Bhoot: It is worthy of notice that some times bhoot is used as a generic term and includes all kinds of spirits. But there is also a specific class named bhoot. They are skilled in changing shapes.

(9) Khetar: The word comes from the Sanskrit khetra, a field, which again is an abbreviation of khetrapala, a presiding spirit of the field. This spirit lives in an open place. He deals particularly with little folks. A large number of children are annually carried off by him. There is another class of khetar, whose business is to take off a newborn calf and keep it concealed. If however as a precautionary, measure a quantity of the milk of the cow thickened by heating be parceled off, and bits put on the ears, neck and loins of the calf and of its mother, the khetar eats them, and, being satisfied, he desists from his mischievous designs.

(10) Markuchia: He spoils a child in the womb of its mother. This generally happens in the third or fourth month of pregnancy. The spirit possesses a girl if she happens to get her first menstruation in an inauspicious moment. If the spirit fails to spoil the child in the womb he pursues it further, and torments it in numerous ways, when it is born.

(11) Prasuta: This is a female spirit. She possesses a pregnant woman.

(12) Kandh: He is a. horrible demon with headless trunk and two furious eyes set upon the breast. He lives on the sea-shore. He wanders about in the country at night and returns to his home at the approach of dawn. He makes frequent awful shrieks from his wind-pipe during his nightly wanderings. The word kandh is derived from the Sanskrit "kabandha," an order of spiritual beings.

(13) Bira: Biras are said to be a class of khetars, but more dreadful. It is very hard to save a man from the grip of this monster.

(14) Panimangali: A person when possessed by this spirit

12

is seized with fever which grows severe in the end. The spirit at this stage breaks some of his victim's limbs and leaves him alone. The victim now finds to his chagrin that though his fever is no more, he is a crippled man.

(15) Parooa: This is a sprightly female spirit. She amuses herself at the meeting of three roads, and leads wayfarers astray if she happens to meet with any. She plays on a musical instrument called taka, which the Assamese girls use, the sound being distinctly audible by men. The traveler losing his way mistakes her voice for that of a man in a distant place and follows it only to find himself forlorn and lost the more, there being none to welcome him. When she wishes to lead a man away she creates a thick mist all around him which makes him see everything indistinct and lose his way. I fancy parooa is a corruption of the Sanskrit pari- a nymph.

(C) Household Spirits:

(1) Ghar-jeuti: The word literally means "light of the house". This is a benign female spirit who presides over a man's house. She is heard to make ticking sounds in the house. When a man happens to sleep at night across the doorway she treads on his body on her way out of or into the house, and the man feels the treading as that of a cat passing over him.

III Aerial spirit: Bardaischila

(l) Bardaischila: She is a female spirit and lives with her husband in a far-off land. She visits her parents' home, which lies in this part of the country, once a year to enjoy the national festival of Baihag Bihu. She returns when the Bihu is ended. We have thus in Assam two strong gales, one just before and the other just after the Bihu, occasioned by the flight of the airy spirit on her journey to and from her parents' home. When she comes in, as can naturally be expected, she is serene and delightful, but on her return voyage she becomes turbulent. Thus the preceding gale is harmless, while the after-gale is destructive, overthrowing trees, razing houses and doing other mischief.

II. A. (b) (Continued)

Jalkoar: This is a. spirit who presides over river. He corresponds to the Sanskrit god Varunu.

II. B (16)

Khabis: He is a Mahommedan spirit, but is found occasionally to possess a Hindu.

(17) Thalgiri or Thalsai: Every locality has a presiding spirit of its own called Thalgiri "master of land," or Thalsai, "god of land."

IV. Celestial spirits: Siva, Jam, Bihkaram, Durga, Kalika, Deo, Lakhima, Bijuli

(1) Siva: He is the great Sanskrit god and worshiped as such. Besides exercising the functions assigned; to him by the Vedas he is supposed by the Assamese to preside over elephants. The keepers have to propitiate him when these beasts are visited with any disaster. This belief may have taken root from the mythical Hindu tale that Ganesh, Siva's son, was a god with the head of an elephant. Siva and his wife are also regarded as nuptial deities.

(2) Jam: He is the Sanskrit god of death. He rides on a buffalo. His legs are believed by the Assamese to be heavy with elephantiasis.

ASSAMESE DEMONOLOGY

(3) Bihkaram: The word is derived from the Sanskrit Biswakarmi, the heavenly architect. He is best known by Assamese women who show great reverence for him. He presides over the weaving looms which they hold so dear.

(4) Durga: She is the wife of Siva, and a familiar deity among the Assamese. She causes measles or small-pox. When a man is seized by her regular services are held by a number of women to propitiate her. There are numerous other names by which she is known among them,, e.g. Sitala, Mahamaya, Bhagawati, Ai, etc. The vernacular name for small pox is ai-olowa (the visitation of the mother).

(5) Kalika: This is another name of the goddess Kali. But her function as kalika is of a different order. She resides in anything grand, a man or an animal or even an inanimate thing for the matter of that. A spotless righteous soul, an unusually tall portly individual, a grand beautiful feathered peacock, a bearded majestic lien, an awful gigantic tusker, an overhanging huge stone, a. turbulent river, the foremost fish in the shoal, traveling up-stream during the rains- these and such like are the usual resorts of kalika.

(6) Deo: Deo is a vulgar term for the goddess Kali. Under her inspiration a man, who is then called a den, is imbued with a high amount of enthusiasm. During this period, he is endowed with the power of presaging future events Pigeons, ducks and goats are sacrificed to the deo, who actually drinks their blood.

(7) Lakhimi: She is the same as Lakshmi, the Sanskrit goddess of plenty. She resides in a house where peace and purity, reign. She resides also in a rice-field. In fact she is identified with rice itself. The first chaff of the crop is carried and deposited in the granary with a ceremony be fitting the goddess.

ari: She is the Sanskrit Apshari, a celestial
punishment to a man for his transgressions.
he ban becomes weaker every day until she is
 once she is named "withering apechari." It would
an offense to tread on the shadow, which falls on the earth but
cannot be seen by mortal eyes, of an apechari in the heaven, and
the offender would be punished as above for so doing.

(9) Bijuli: Bijuli is the goddess, Lightning. She is a
passingly handsome maiden, and the lightning is the flash of her
inimitable naked person.

I. Subterranean spirits: Goolai.

Goolai: He is a spirit who presides over buried treasure.
He comes out in the shape of an adjutant bird, and Wanders
about at night in search of food. In the beak of this bird there
burns a fire which shows him the way.

IV. (11) (Continued).

It is said that a "shooting star" is a man who after his
death lived in heaven in the good graces of an apechari, but who
has now been hurled down by his sweet companion, his period of
bliss having expired.

ASSAMESE DEMONOLOGY

CHAPTER II: INCANTATIONS AND EXPULSION OF SPIRITS

Let me at the beginning give an account of the symptoms of possession by some of the spirits.

Peret: The victim is afflicted with itches, boils, etc., or has an attack of quartian fever.

Chamon: The eyes of the victim turn yellow. His face is flushed.

Alakhani: The victim has a painful aching sensation in his stomach.

Bura Dangaria: The victim feels pain in the head, chest, waist and limbs. The pain is so acute that the man has not the power to stoop.

Khetar: The victim who is a child is attacked with convulsive fits. A male khetar possesses even an adult man during sleep, causing him to groan and utter distressing sounds.

Prasuta: The victim who is a pregnant woman is seized with fever. She suffers from swelling of the limbs. She feels always drowsy. A woman possessed by prasuda is afflicted with other painful symptoms also.

Datial, or Jankakharia: The victim suffers from very high fever attended with aching pain in both temples. This may; last for ten days or so.

Panimangali: The eyes of the victim turn red. He behaves stupidly, grasps aimlessly with his hands and plays with

17

sweepings, rags, dust, etc.

Bhoot: The victim suffers from an acute attack of fever.

Alakhani: The victim feels as if a stone were forcing its way up into his heart from his stomach, and is greatly pained. When possessed by a male alakhani he becomes almost unconscious with agony for a time.

The following books of incantations are used to expel spirits: Karsala Ban, Bishnu Ban, Saria Ban, Kher Ban, Rudra Ban, Chakra Ban. Let me describe some of the methods of exorcism with the above books:

(a) KarsalaBan: Karsala is a kind of grass. The possessed man is struck with this grass, duly enchanted. The spirit then makes his retreat.

(b) Guburua Ban: Literally a "beetle arrow." Three beetles are killed and squeezed to powder, and are then mixed ceremonially with mustard oil and alkaline water. This mixture, sprinkled on the body; of the possessed man, expels the spirit.

(c) Agni Ban: Literally "fire arrow." A torch is prepared of titabahak twigs, the flame being held up. A quantity of mustard seed is thrown over the fire in such manner that sparks are let off and fall on the body of the possessed man, the usual incantations being repeated in the meantime.

(d) Jal Ban: Literally "water arrow". The rib of a dried plantain leaf is burnt to ashes which are mixed with a quantity of bubble-bubble water. The mixture being sprinkled on the eyes (if the possessed man with proper incantations makes the spirit retire.

(e) Kharika Ban: Literally "arrow of thatching grass." A quantity of thatching grass is enchanted and cast on the body of the possessed man, when the spirit runs away.

(f) Bishnu Ban: Garlic, onion and certain other medicinal roots are pulverized, and mixed with mustard oil and and water. The mixture is sprinkled on the body of the possessed man with proper incantations. The spirit then leaves the victim and repairs to his haunt.

(g) Sariah Ban: Literally "mustard arrow." The exorcist takes a quantity of mustard seeds in his mouth and blows them towards the possessed man through a sieve placed in front of him, uttering certain incantations mean while. The mustard falling on the possessed man causes a burning sensation. The spirit unable to bear the pain leaves his victim.

(h) Kher Ban: Literally "straw arrow." A quantity of straw duly enchanted is thrown at the possessed man. This, when it hits him, makes the spirit fly for life.

(I) Rudra Ban: Mustard seeds, orris and certain other medicinal roots are pulverized and mixed diluted with mustard oil. The mixture when sprinkled on the man's eyes makes the spirit depart to the place from Which it came.

(J) Chakra Ban: The mode of exorcism is much the same as the above. In time of emergency the exorcist uses only short incantations called dikhas. The following dikhas are in use: Sani Dikha, Kal Dikha, Rudra Dikha, Nara Dikha, Singha Dikha, Brahma Dikha.

The following are some of the principal books of incantations, used to expel spirits: Adi Nara Singha, Chausasthi Nara Singha, Ajapa Nara Singha, Balia Nara Singha, Samudia,

ASSAMESE DEMONOLOGY

Pakshiraj, Garuri, Bilahi Bejini, Garbha-Dharan, Kanchan, Kalap, Pani Bejini.

To expel a khetar from the body of a woman the following medicine is used, proper incantations being repeated during the preparation:

(a) Water drawn from seven different ghats.
(b) Oil collected from seven different shops.
(c) Bent-grass.
(d) Rice prepared from paddy dried in the sun.

These are mixed together. A mystic thread is prepared and is dipped in the mixture. The woman drinks the mixture and wears the mystic thread on her neck. In the event of the exorcist having to deal with a formidable spirit he employs the following method: He puts a quantity of chili seeds and mustard grain inside a fruit and by blowing it with his mouth forces them out. This makes the possessed man sneeze. The spirit then says through the mouth of the possessed man that he is ready to go if a puja is offered. This is done, and the spirit true to his word, leaves the man. Let me observe *en passant* that sneezing by the person operated on is, in this mode of exorcism, considered to be a sure sign of possession. Another test of possession is that the man becomes restless when made to lie down on a leaf of a bar-kachu plant duly enchanted. Possession is also indicated by a certain number of bel leaves pressed against the navel of the man engendering an amount of pain which he cannot bear.

Besides the Hindu spirits, khabish, which is a muslim spirit, is also seen to possess a man, as said above. In that case, he is expelled by means of the ordinary Hindu incantation with only this exception, that instead of a Hindu god the name of the Muhammadan divinity Allah occurs at the end of each verse.

20

ASSAMESE DEMONOLOGY

When the mystic thread is prepared there are certain signs by which it can be known whether the possessed man will survive or succumb. If the mixture of oil and water with which the mystic thread is anointed turn white the man will come round. Should it however turn black the man will die. If the upper end of the mystic thread be found shorter than the lower end the victim is almost sure to die. Besides the books of incantations referred to in another place, there is another book called "sleeping arrow" (Nidra-Ban): No particular mode of exorcism is described in it. It contains incantations, which, when repeated causes the possessed man to fall into a slumber during which the exorcist gains sufficient time to prepare for the spectral warfare.

In the case of pregnant woman possessed by markuchia, the victim gets fever, burning sensation and looseness of bowels. The embryo is then spoiled. She recovers however when proper incantations are repeated or a mystic thread is used. This spirit has to be expelled in the third or fifth month of pregnancy or else it is hard to save the child when born from his fatal grip.

A whip being enchanted is allowed freedom of movements, a man holding it in his hand. He is a mere tool subservient to the command of the whip. The whip then goes and strikes the victim mercilessly until the spirit makes a clean breast and says who is he, why he is there and what he wants. Proper offerings being provided he goes and the man is himself again. The exorcist asks the spirit to show a visible sign by which all may be sure of his departure. The spirit then breaks off a twig of the nearest tree in shows whatever sign the exorcist asks him to show. When a spirit possesses a man a quantity of hair of his head is tied into a knot by any layman, who then addressing the spirit names the exorcist whom he intends to call. If the spirit knows him to be too powerful. for him, he turns tail, grows restless and asks to have the exorcist brought in at once.

CHAPTER III: SUPPLEMENTARY NOTES

1. The spirit fears the rifle. Hence in a case of ghostly phenomenon we hear of volleys of fire. It is known to all that elephant-keepers when out in the forest fire their rifles to scare away spirits.

2; Instances of domesticated ghosts are not rare. These live in the shape of common rats. When the master seeks to punish an enemy he summons them, puts them inside an earthen pot, stealthily walks into his enemy's house and lets the rats loose unnoticed by anybody. The rats entering into the belly of the man, of course mystically, set themselves to eat into his vitals, leading him eventually into death.

3. When a dot lives in a bamboo clump and wants to frighten a passer-by, he shakes the bamboo as a strong blast would. But curiously enough not a single bamboo is blown down.

4. The khetar has long teeth like spikes. Sometimes he assumes horrible shapes, when the poor child, his victim, gets frightened and weeps, Sometimes he bursts into laughter, when the child takes the infection and laughs with. Him.

5. A mystic takes a number of duck eggs to a graveyard and there lays them in a cavity dug upon a grave on a Saturday or a Tuesday. After a Period of three days the eggs are brought back and kept inside a cotton bale, where they are hatched in due course. The ofispring are however rats, not ducklings. These rats must always be satisfied with suitable offerings of food and drink, or else the master runs the risk of being himself destroyed by his own proteges.

6. The kandh has two eyes set upon the breast which sparkle like the eyes of a. fierce tiger. He wanders about dancing a hideous dance. Sometimes he is seen to dart at full speed with outbursts of horrible laughter and unearthly shrieks.

7. The spectral bag of the dot is a round little thing made of net cloth.

8. Besides incantations the dot is afraid of weapons of iron. The rest of the spirits can be conquered by incantations only.

9. The dot and bak do not generally kill a man. They belabor him mercilessly and leave him alone to shift for himself as best he can. The Bhoot assumes different shapes and enters into the body of the victim after frightening him. It is the khetar who is most skilled in the art of changing his shape. The chamon and the jakh are not good. at this, while markuchia is a moderate performer.

10. The spirits have dialect of their own, e.g., a. chamon has: Ban-bhungka-uka for a dog. Jerjerua-uka for a fowl. Hemai-ai-uka for a pig.

When a chamon possessing a man is questioned by the exorcist as to what he means to do, he replies in his appropriate tongue.

11. The spirits have wives and children like men. They have no hierarchy of castes among them.

12. The dot and the bak visit stealthily the fishing traps set by men and eat the fish caught in. them. They are sometimes seen to be so audacious as to eat silk cocoons out of a bag while it is being carried by a man. They also eat shells.

13. A jakhini dances and makes gestures. She does not sing.

14. Sometimes a. male khetar visits a Woman and a female khetar a man. They make illicit proposals. If the man or the woman as the case may be accepts the proposal, the spirit takes away in the act the life-blood of the victim who is led as a result into wreckage and ultimate death.

15 The spirits cast no shadow on the ground as men do.

16. A spirit has only one wife. A female spirit has only one husband. Adultery is not allowed.

17. In certain cases the spirit recites the very incantations which the exorcist is about to recite, and taunts, him in other ways.

18. A dot is sometimes seen to come to a market and make purchases in the shape of an ordinary man.

19. To propitiate the nymph apechari the women of the locality assemble and hold a service, offering a quantity of powdered rice and nine bunches of plantains.

20. The spirit kills the exorcist when his ill-luck would so have it. All exorcists have to live under constant fear of devils, who seek opportunity to injure them. A spirit has been heard to say to his exorcist: "I am here to kill this man. Surely you meddle in an evil hour."

21. The spirit who takes a woman away does not keep her always but sends her back to her home. She is in this way restored after being kidnapped.

22. Mayang is a mouza, lying in the district of Now-gong. It has been noted for witchcraft for years. The people keep daini and other spirits in their houses. They send. them to any man whom they want to injure. They bring good things from other houses by sending a daini. This emissary is offered a pooja, and is sent out on her mission with these words; "Back when I bid you. Away with my enemy unless he calls on me and satisfies my demand." The people have places reserved in the dark secluded part of their houses for pooja to the ghosts. I note below some of the preternatural doings of the Mayang people.

(a) The half-burnt wooden pegs on which the cooking pot is rested take root, and the rice is never done although the fire is full-fed.

(b) A man's seat sticks to him, and does not drop off until the mystic recites counter-incantations.

(c) A tree stands although cut through, and falls only when the enemy whom the mystic wishes to injure comes up to it.

(d) A cooked pigeon when eaten becomes alive inside the stomach, and flapping its wings incessantly kills the man. I

(e) When a man eats rice and milk this is never digested but takes root in the stomach. He dies within six months.

(f) A rib of a plantain leaf is turned into a snake.

(a) The leaves of the saura tree are turned into khaliha and kawai fishes. The mystic keeps a number of ghosts. These are constantly coming in and going out on their errands by turns. The usual method of destruction by a daini is that the victim is subjected to an acute form of dysentery. The disease grows severer every day, and the man ultimately dies.

CHAPTER IV: STORIES

1. In Golaghat there is a family whose forefathers were reputed to be ghost-keepers. They are still known as the "house of ghosts." The matron of-the house had charge of them. The ghosts lived in a mango tree in the orchard, and when they came down. from it assumed the shape of rats or kindred small creatures, ate food offered by their mistress, all in a pell-mell fashion, and returned to their haunt.

2. Once a daini assuming the form of a woman met a traveler and bore him company, keeping behind him. She irresistibly felt the temptation of eating human flesh, so much so that her lips protruded. These however she advisedly reverted to their normal size by rubbing them against her arm. The man happened to look back and saw that it was a fiend that followed him. The daini, perceiving that the cat was out of the bag, disappeared.

3. A chamon was walking slowly in the shape of a Naga, heavily laden with a basket on his back. He accosted a man, and said; "Tell my eldest brother his wife is dead." He also gave the address of his brothers, said to be six in number, as a certain huge tree in a particular locality. The man could see no house in the place mentioned, but he shouted so as to be heard far and wide- "The wife of the eldest brother is dead. Know ye whomsoever it may concern." Suddenly a blast shook the tree, and piteous wailings rent the sky. The traveler understood the import and hastened his way homeward.

4. There are twelve scores of jakh in the Barpeta Bil in Nowgong. A notable bhakat named Baloram Deori lived in the satra. For an offense against piety he became a jakh on his death, and proceeded to the Barpeta Bil. But the other jakhs dubbed

27

him the blackest devil as having committed an offense against piety, and refused him admittance. Many bhakats seeing his pitiable position argued his cause, but to no purpose. The gossain himself came to the scene. The newly arrived jakh recounted the facts, and added that he was sentenced to live with jakhs for one year. Out of compassion the good gossain reduced the sentence to six months, and ordered the resident jakhs to allow him a place in the bile

5. A man was calling his brother Banmali by name when suddenly a ghost appeared before him and began to laugh aloud. After a while he paused and said: 'Ban dhamalil What a nice name! If this should ever reach the ear of my four brothers, whose names are;

> the filth of a duck,
> the feather of a pigeon,
> the filth of an otter,
> a broken khampi,
> they will laugh and laugh till their sides split.'

6. A man once saw a pisachani sitting as a wretchedly dressed gray-haired old woman absorbed in thought, with the palm of her hand pressed against her head.

7. A man once saw a nautch party held by five alak-hanis Three of them clapped their hands and the other two danced to the music.

8. A man was sleeping one night across his door-way. A gharjeuti came near in the shape of a baby of about two years and tried to pass over him but suddenly paused. In this way there was a continual process of attempt and pause, until after a time the man awoke. He removed his bed from the doorway.

9. Two brothers were out in a boat fishing in a river. The younger brother held the net at the bow, while the elder sat at the helm. A dot came, killed the elder brother, himself assumed his shape and steered the boat as before, the younger brother having no knowledge whatever of the ghostly interference. Many fishes were caught by the younger brother and deposited in the boat, but these the dot kept on eating secretly all the while. The younger brother noticed the low level of the fish, and realized that something had happened to his brother. But he very prudently went on as if nothing had happened. The dot was outwitted. He took the man for a simpleton, and putting confidence in him handed over his spectral bag to him for custody. Taking the bag in his hand the younger brother said to the dot; "You are at my, mercy, you miserable wretch!" The man thought within himself that it would not be wise to give out the melancholy news of his brother's death, especially when he could manage to. make the spirit pass for his brother. He and the spirit went home together and lived peaceably as brothers, none else having the slightest inkling of what had taken place. The younger brother kept the spectral bag in a mustard barn. Time passed, and the spirit kept on trying all sorts of means to obtain the bag if possible. At last it so happened that the younger brother attended a mel, at a distance. The dot also started for the mel, but hurried back to the home and said to his victim's mother: "The bag! The bag! The bag in the mustard barn. Plenty of coins in the mel. Well, where's the place for them." The simple mother took him at his word and gave him the bag The dot took the bag, became himself again, and proceeded to the woods. The younger brother returned from the mel His mother said, "Where is your brother? I gave him the bag that was in the mustard barn." Her son sighed a deep sigh and said "Know, poor mother, your eldest son died the moment you gave up the bag." So saying he recounted the sad incident of his brother's death from start to finish.

10. A dot visited a Brahmin girl in the form of her lover and eloped with her. In course of time she became the mother of two children by the dot. A little before the birth of the third child the woman asked him to procure her a fish from a certain distant place as she desired to eat one. The dot set out to get the fish, and meantime the woman with her sons, seizing this opportunity of her spirit-husband's absence, hastened to her parents' home. The dot returned with a fish but found no one in his house. He traced the woman to her parent's house, the fish still in his hand. He got on the roof, made an opening and dropping the fish through saying: "Take it, inconstancy thy nature." Then he retraced his steps homewards. The limbs of this woman's sons were sluggish and bore long streaks all over like those of a spirit.

11. The dot fears a fish-hook. Once as a dot was trying to eat a fish out of a bag carried by a man on his back he got entangled in the fishing line and the hook pierced his belly. The dot being thus enslaved obtained release by abject entreaties.

12 A ghost assumed the shape of an old man and visited his house in his absence. He stood on the courtyard and asked the wife to wash his feet. They were smooth, unlike those of her old husband which the wife knew to be rugged. She suspected something was wrong, looked up and saw a very tall figure. At once she entered the house on the pretext of bringing more water, bolted the door and screamed. The spirit said: "You are lucky, you are lucky;" and vanished into thin air.

13. A ghost appeared to a man in a dream and said: "Keep your young daughter on the grass upon a cloth' spread out. I shall come and take her away, and in exchange will put on the cloth plenty of riches for you." The man did not comply with this request, as was to be expected. The girl died in less than a week.

14., There was a commotion recently in Golaghat owing to the appearance of a ghost in the house of one Dewai Tekela in village Khangia, mauza Naharani. The ghost stayed in the house for three years. People from distant places visited the house, and after due inquiry were satisfied with the genuineness of this incident. The visitation of the ghost had particular reference to a married girl of sixteen. Her husband was living with her. Clods of earth used to be thrown at her by the ghost. She could actually see him although no one else did. She was never kidnapped by him, and he never molested her while she stayed at her father's house. Her father-in-law died a year before this incident. The ghost said to him: "I am your father-in-law. I come to see you out of love."

The ghost occasionally played pranks. He concealed cups and plates, and even valuable ornaments. But he was sometimes useful. He looked to the comfort of the guests and provided them with seats, pan, etc. But when any guest insulted him he scattered bhat over him. When bhat was served to a member of the family the ghost ate it up before curry arrived. The cook took the hint, reserved a dish specially for the ghost, and then all annoyance ceased. The bhat disappeared from the reserved dish in the sight of all men.

15. The Hindu god Siva lived in mount. Kailas with his wife Parvati. Lakshmi, the goddess of wealth and the wife of Vishnu, paid a visit to Parvati when Siva was absent. During the course of conversation Lakshmi referred to Siva. slightingly, he being but a beggar after all. Parvati in reply expressed her contempt for Vishnu. Lakshmi game home and related to her husband what had happened. Vishnu who knew well that Siva's poverty was the result of hisunparallelled piety and absolute indifierence to temporal possessions, said to. Lakshmi "Let me devise a means by which Parvati will be humiliated. At the same time there will be plenty of harvest for men to eat on earth." He

31

commanded four Siddhas to visit Siva's house during the absence of the latter, and on some pretext to ask for a quantity of rice. These immediately hurried to Kailas and asked Parvati for some rice, so that they might refresh themselves after so tire some a journey. Parvati finding not a grain of rice in her house gave them some fruits to eat. The guests departed, but Parvati felt humiliated. When Siva came home she asked him to procure the necessary implements of agriculture and to grow rice. She advised him to obtain a plot of land from Indra, a bag of rice seedlings from Kuvera, and a plow from Baloram. The rope of Varuna was to be his plow-rope, the Chakra of Vishnu his yoke, and the serpent Basuki his whip. He was instructed to get the buffalo of yama and yoke it with his own bullock.

His trident was to be his plow-share. His son Kartik was to be his plow-boy. Parvati herself was to cook the rice. Siva was well pleased and accepted the suggestions of his wife. He collected all the implements of husbandry and began at cock-crow to cultivate his field. He was so absorbed in his new occupation that he ignored the calls of appetite. When it was past noon, Parvati created a body of mosquitoes and wasps and commanded them to invade the field so that Siva might leave the plow and come home. Siva seeing the fierce onset made a torch and whirled it violently so that the insects fled for their lives, Parvati finding that her object failed, created an army of earth-worms, leeches, rats, and crickets but Siva was too much engrossed in his business to mind such annoyances. Parvati now proceeded in person to find her husband. She found the field covered with all manner of crops in various stages of growth. But as soon as her indignant eyes fell upon the crops there came out from her mouth a demon and a demoness named Khob and Khubi, who set the whole field in a blaze. Siva turned back and seeing the couple of fiends wanted to kill them. They prayed for mercy and added that as they were the offspring of his wifes' mind it behooved him to spare their lives. Siva admitted this, but told them to leave the field at once and take up their residence in the Dhedheya Hills. With regard to the question of food he said. "Be in the mouths of men horn in inauspicious moments and eat your food there." Siva and Pérvati returned home.

Ages passed, and Rama's faithful attendant Hanuman took the Dhedheya Hills among others to bridge the sea. Khob and Khubi who were in the Hills went with them. They entreated Rama, allow them a country to live in and suitable food to subsist on. Rama directed them to live among men and to eat the food assigned to them by Siva. He gave them also something more. He said: "Live with the bridegroom till the third day of marriage, when a service will take place in which vegetables will be distributed among those assembled. Eat enough, and leave the couple to themselves."

The custom of holding the above service in which a Brahmin priest recounts the story of Khob and Khubi to the married couple is universal with the Assamese.

The story of Khob and Khubi originally appeared in the Nandi Purana, from which it has been translated into Assamese.

The crop, which was burnt by the appearance of Khob and Khubi, came to be known as aim, the other being stilt which is the staple crop of the Assamese.

16. There lived a king who had a. beautiful wife named Kamala. His kingdom was visited by intense drought and many lives were lost. Jalkoer who was smitten with the beauty of the queen, appeared in a dream to the king, and said that he would send water if the king would part with his consort. The king at first refused, but when the drought continued and the people implored him to save their lives at any cost he yielded. The people

excavated a tank and the queen proceeded to it in a magnificent procession, followed by the king and by immense crowds. The queen went down into the tank. The king stood on the bank, and as the water gradually rose the following conversation ensued:

> "How much water do you meet,
> Say Kamala my consort sweet
> Harken ye, my husband dear,
> Water is now ankle near.
> How much water do you find,
> Say Kamala, ever kind.
> My beloved lord, list ye,
> Water kisses now my knee.
>
> How much water does now spring,
> Say unto me, my darling.
> My lord, on heart enthroned high,
> Water has now reached my thigh.
> My heart, Kamala, breaks for thee,
> O, say, how much water you see.
> My sweet master, shed not tear,
> Water is now loin near.
>
> Ah me! Hear my mournful lay,
> How much water rushes, say.
> Is not fate supreme yet found?
> Water ties my breast around.
> Be not sad, my queen of spring,
> How much water does jalkoer bring.
> All is o'er, I bow to thee!
> Water encircles my neck, now see."

Suddenly a golden barge appeared and the queen was taken on board and vanished from sight.

APPENDIX I: SONG OF ALAKHANI

Tick, tick tita'pat
It rains, there's mire
Ah me! men will see.
But what may they say!

APPENDIX II: INCANTATION USED IN WEAVING SPECTRAL THREAD

I Salute Thee, O Krishna.
One, I bind the eleven.
Two, I bind the two directions.
Three, I bind the triangular earth.
Four, I bind the four cardinal points.
Five, I bind the five demons.
Six, I bind the sixty-four gipsies.
Seven, I bind the hundred stars.
Eight, I bind the eight ghats.
Nine, I bind the nine stars.
Ten, I bind the lord of ten directions.
Eleven, I bind the eleven mothers.
Twelve, I bind the motley crowd.
Thirteen, I bind the thirteen celestial nymphs.
Fourteen, I bind fourteen phases of the moon.
Fifteen, I bind the fifteen stars.
Sixteen, I bind the sixteen ghats.
Seventeen, I bind the seventeen moons.
Eighteen, I bind the eighteen pathways.
Nineteen, I bind the nineteen gha's.
Twenty, I bind the ten gates.

Should none these avail,
I bind by the sixty-four incantations.

Siva himself on the east rampart,
The sun, the west rampart,
Death himself, out of compassion, on the south.
Durga on the north rampart.
Should my words come to grief.
The purity of the goddess will be dashed off.
By my adjuration, and my preceptor's command,
Remain where I bind.

APPENDIX III: PRINCIPAL HAUNTED PLACES

Nowgong

> Barpeta Bil
> Hahila JaJah
> Jamuna Jalah
> Silabandha Bil
> Malaha Bil
> Bamun Gossain Than
> Barhampur Pukhuri
> Leli. Bar
> Moeaari Kurk

Jorhat

> Padumani Bil
> Hekera Kurh
> Barbarua Korokani
> Hizalguri Pukhuri
> Jagdooar
> Kaliapani
> Rangapani Pathar
> Charaipani Jan
> Barbheta Dopani
> Adhakhana Barpukhuri

ASSAMESE DEMONOLOGY

Phatikar Chiga pool
Malow Pathar
Kaliani Pathar
Bbarmukali Pathar

Mangaldai

Burinagar Pukhuri
Barhampur Pukhuri
Gorakata Pukhuri
Jaypal Pukhuri
Bhurar Garh
Deomara Nai Jar

Gauhati

Sandhya Jar
Changchaki Pahar
Kohora Garh
Balilecha Pukhuri
Kalagarh Pukhuri

Barpeta

Sundari Bil.
Enger Pora Kurh.
Baghar Parbat
Chakutal Joa
Pithakatia Pukhuri
Panisala Pukhuri

Golaghat

Khecheng Bar
Semetia Bar

Kaliapani Bar
Na-Bil
Malar Chiga Barghuli
Rahdhala Pukhuri.
Naga pota Bar

Sibsagar

Singi Bil
Mitangar Dalang
Sing-Duar
Kuji-Bali
Gar Gaon
Phulpani Chiga
Talatali Gh'ar
Jai Sagar
Gauri Sager
Athai Sager
Na-Pukhuri

Dibrugarh

Tapa Pool
Aithan
Raja Bheta Jan
Merbil
Sissimukh

North Lakhimpur

Nata Kana Bari Pukhuri.
Pitani Pukhuri.
Rahdhala Pukhuri.
Garia Jan
Gharmarar Chola

Khana Pukhuri
Kandali Pukhuri

Tezpur

Molan Pukhuri
Kini Pukhuri
Uhani
Naharlaga. Jarani
Kuari Pukhuri
Baralimara Bil
Syam Narayan Pukhuri

APPENDIX IV: NOTABLE EXORCISTS

North Lakhimpur

Jaduram Sarma

Dibrugarh.

Khora Bez
Bihua Bez
Bhadram Sarma

Jorhat

Bapiram Sarma
Dutiraim Bardalai
Bhaibiraim Barua
Domai Koch
Sambhu Nath Mahanta
Ghana Kanta Sarma
Soneram Sarma.
Parapati Sarabjan

Sonaram Mahari
Bapirzim Chutia
Khetekeswar Sarma

Barpeta

Sukhna Khora
Narayan Bamun
Ghosaram
Mihiram
Gobindram

Golaghat.

Bagidia Medhi
Dutiram Gaonbura
Katie Bez
Mukund Chutia
Barkathia Keot
Datram Pandit
Ramakanta Gagar
Bihua Sarma
Gopinath Gohain
Aniram Pandit
Makara Bez
Bharam Gaonbura

Sibsagar

Krishnaram Kalita
Madhuram Ganak
Kathak Bez
Paoli Bez
Mukti Kalitu
Arjun Deodhai

Haribar Kohar
Mani Charingie

Tezpur

Bilai Kalita
Mim Garia
Jogeswar Barua
Mani Pandit
Kerkan Mandal
Gopi Satola
Maria Kalita

Nowgong

Kirtinath Sarma
Phaguna Koch
Manika Sarma Tamuli
Bhumidhar Sarma Barua
Chenaram Sarma Tamuli
Rameswar Koch
Gerela Keot
Doyaram Koch

Gauhati

Ganeswar Sarma

GLOSSARY

Ahu: A species of early rice which is reaped at the end of the rainy season.

Ban: The Indian fig tree.

Bar Kachu: A species of arum.

Bah: A kind of fruit with valuable medicinal properties.

Bhakat: A disciple of a religious preceptor.

Bhat: Boiled rice.

Bihu: There are three well known Assamese festivals called Bihu. These are distinguished by prefixing the name of the month in which they occur, Magh Bihu, Chait or Baihag Bihu, and Kati Bihu. The Baihag Bihu is the Assamese new year.

Bil: A lake or swamp.

Chakra: The wheel of Vishnu.

Chiga: A breach.

Dalang: A bridge.

Garh: An embankment.

Ghat: -Step to approach a river or a tank.

Ghuli: A pool.

ASSAMESE DEMONOLOGY

Gossain: religious preceptor.

Jalah: A large pool of water.

Jan: A grove.

Jhampi: An Assamese umbrella made of woven palm leaves.

Jika: The cornered gourd. (Luffa acutangula.)

Karsala: A long slender grass abundant in Assam.

Kawai: A kind of fish.

Khaliha: A kind 0f fish.

Korokani: Undulating ground.

Kurh: A spring.

Mel: A village assembly.

Naga: Savage tribes inhabiting one frontier of Assam.

Nahanr: A kind of tree. (Mesua ferrea.)

Nautch: A dance.

Pahar: A hill.

Pan: Betel leaf.

Parbat: A mountain.

Pool: A culvert

Puja: Worship. Also an offering to a god or spirit.

Pukhuri.: A tank.

Sali: A species of rice reaped in the winter. It is transplanted, and is the staple crop in Assam.

Sam: A kind of tree. (Artocarpus chaplasha.)

Satra: The place where the adherents of a particular Gossain reside. Some of these orders are celibate, and some are not.

Saura: A kind of tree.

Siddha: An order of spiritual beings.

Taka: A musical instrument made of bamboo used by rustic girls when they dance.

Than: The place where a holy man is buried.

Tita Bahak: A medicinal plant. (Justicia granderussa.)

THE END

31951074R00029

Made in the USA
Lexington, KY
26 February 2019